Numeracy Cornerstones Level 2

The Francis-Campbell Approach

Resource Booklet

Rev. Dr. Natasha R. Francis-Campbell

Numeracy Cornerstones Level 2: The Francis-Campbell Approach Resource Booklet

Published by Jabneh Publishing
Sterling
Grange Hill P.O.
Westmoreland
Jamaica
Telephone: 876 457 4005
Email: jabnehpublishing@gmail.com
Website: www.jabnehpublishing.com

ISBN 978-1-0898-1883-0
For worldwide distribution
Printed in the United States of America

Table of Contents

Let us count.

1	6
2	7
3	8
4	9
5	10

Let us count.

11		**16**	
12		**17**	
13		**18**	
14		**19**	
15		**20**	

1	2	3	4
5	6	7	8
9	10	11	12
13	14	15	16
17	18	19	20

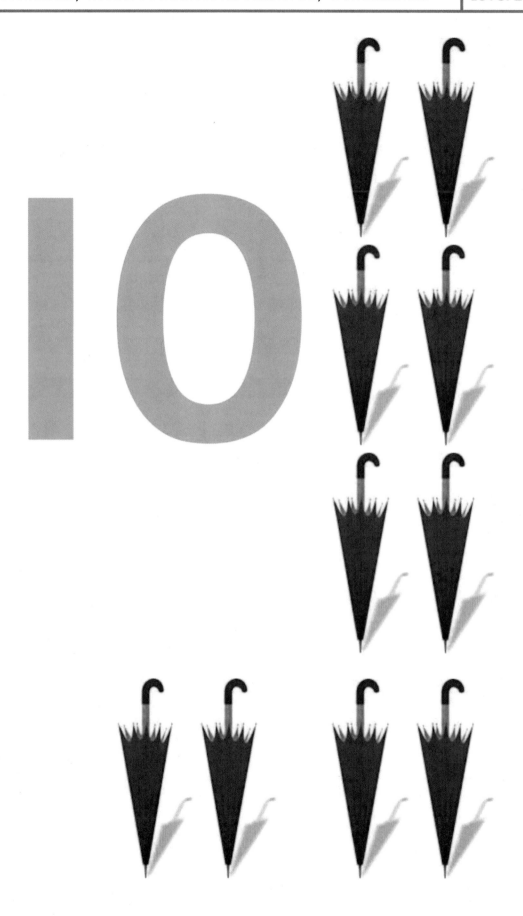

12

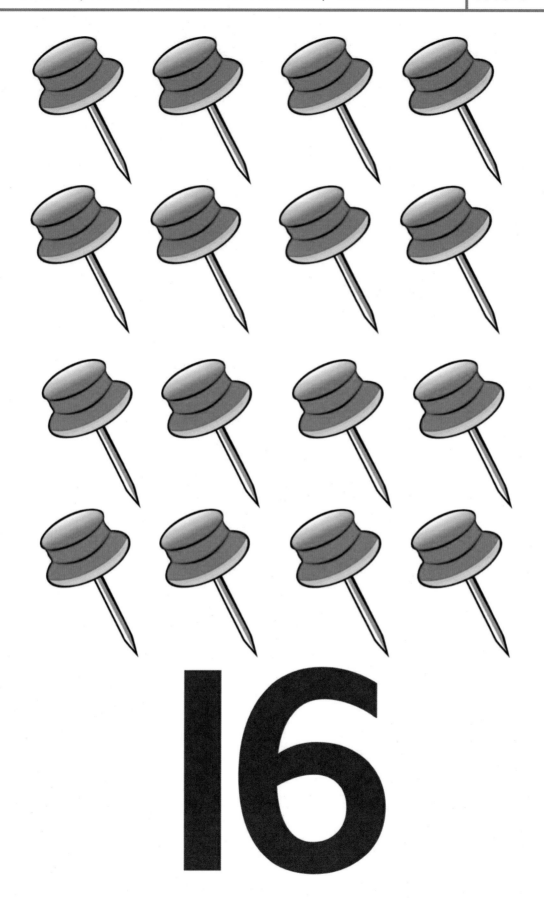

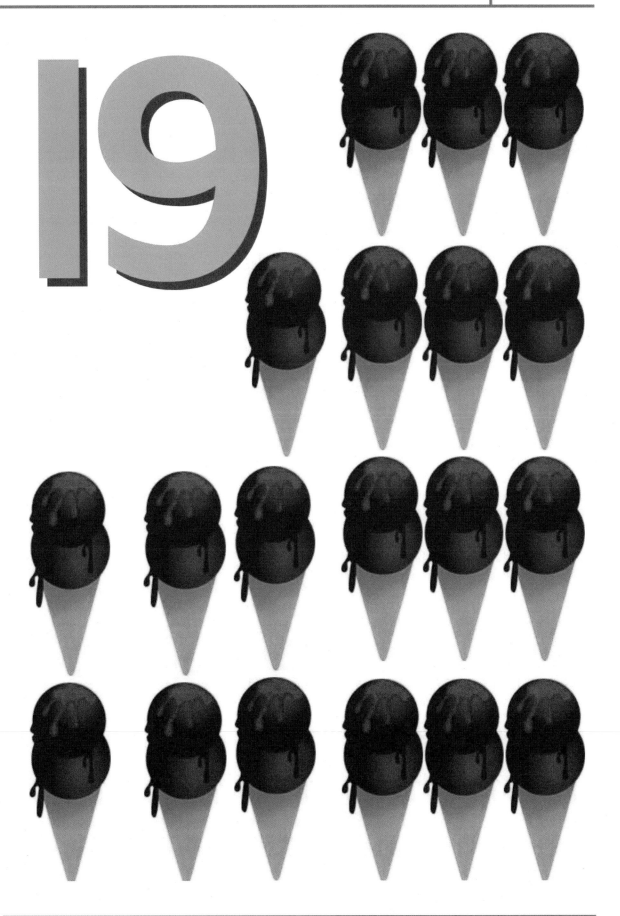

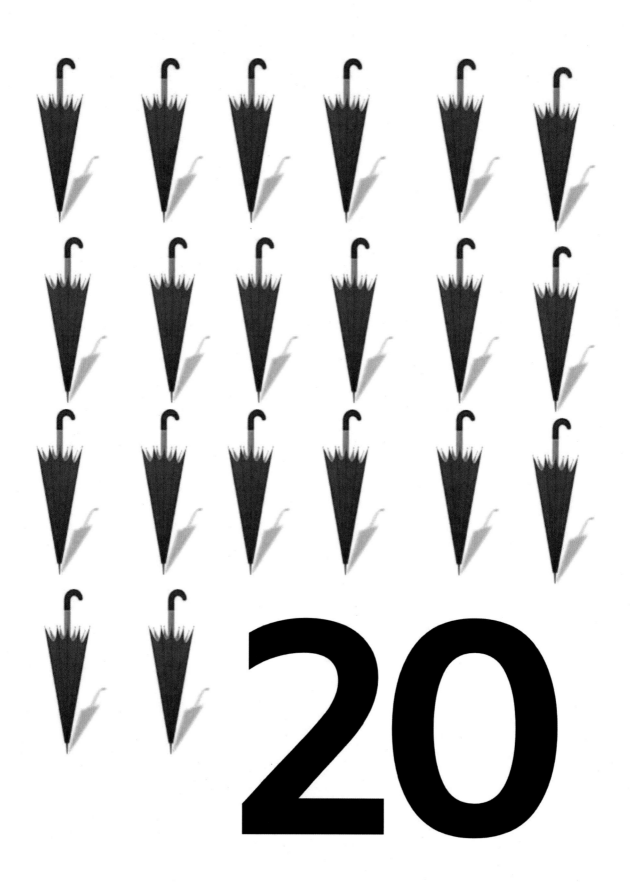

TEEN NUMBERS

13	14
15	16
17	18
19	

The teen family has seven members. Each member of the family of the teen family has the same ending to its name. At the end of each name you will hear "TEEN".

For all the members in the teen family, except 3 and 5, you can call the last digits then add teen.

Let us try.

Twenty Family

20	21
22	23
24	25
26	27
28	29

Money

Money is paper notes and coins that people use to buy things and to pay for services. Here are pictures of some Jamaican money:

The coins and paper notes have numbers on them. These numbers help us to know each coin or paper note value.

Dollar Sign

This symbol means dollar.

The Sum

$$
\begin{array}{r}
5 \\
+4 \\
\hline
9
\end{array}
$$

The answer to an addition problem is called the sum.

This is the cent symbol.

Let us read.

1¢	2¢	3¢	4¢
5¢	6¢	7¢	8¢
9¢	10¢	11¢	12¢
13¢	14¢	15¢	16¢
17¢	18¢	19¢	20¢

Days of the Week

Sunday

Monday

Tuesday

Wednesday

Thursday

Friday

Saturday

How many days?

Months

January	July
February	August
March	September
April	October
May	November
June	December

How many months?

ZERO

Zero means none or nothing.

Let us read.

$$0 + 1 = 1 \qquad 1 + 0 = 1$$

$$0 + 2 = 2 \qquad 2 + 0 = 2$$

$$0 + 3 = 3 \qquad 3 + 0 = 3$$

$$0 + 4 = 4 \qquad 4 + 0 = 4$$

$$0 + 5 = 5 \qquad 5 + 0 = 5$$

$$0 + 6 = 6 \qquad 6 + 0 = 6$$

Quiz Card

1. What number comes after number two?

2. How many fingers and thumbs can you find on one hand?

3. How many days are in one week?

4. What number is this? (Choose and show a number)

5. What number comes before 10?

6. How many apples are in a bag that has one dozen apples?

7. Name a teen number.

8. Which is the smallest teen number?

9. Which is the largest teen number?

10. How many months are in one year?

Shapes

Made in the USA
Monee, IL
08 August 2023

40259372R00021